Poems I and II

Poems by Fred C. Applebaum

ISBN-13: 978-0692692578
ISBN-10: 0692692576

for more books, visit Pski's Porch:
www.pskisporch.com

Printed in U.S.A

with love to Comfortina,
and to everyone else who reads these poems

A Brief Note Concerning Project Applebaum

Gentle reader, please forgive the title of this book, which is inaccurate. It really should be titled Poems II and I, but I don't like the sound of it, so I will follow typical, non-orbital numbering, even though the order of poems herein really is Book 2, followed by Book 1. Also forgive the pseudonymous authorial pose: my legal name is Marc Pietrzykowski, and I write poems under that name as well, but I found myself wanting a different kind of project, one where I could imagine I was someone else, who wrote poems differently. The plan is to add 3 more chapbooks to this collection, at which point the error will be five-fold: Poems I, II, III, IV, and V will actually start with the fifth book and work backward, chronologically to the first.

I hope you enjoy the poems.

Contents

Book II (2016)

Book I (2015)

Afterward

A row
of stunted
pine
wind-bent
penitents
bowing
to the east.

Barn
after
barn
collapsing
on
the horizon
beyond,
ghost
ships
sinking.

In the shorn
field
a farmer
searches
for his
downed
drone.

I am no
prophet
but it seems
the world
is suggesting
we the people
adjourn.

An Oath

On
my
knees
in the
dry
riverbed
crows
witness
from
above
worms
from
below
my
promise
to you:

I
will
live
from
breath
to
breath
present
never

heedless
aware
from
breath
to
breath
that
I am
the sky
the sea
the song
of caves
the mist
clinging
to
hay bales
the tear
on your
cheek
the want
in your
heart.

Crows
and
worms
have
added
their
seal

there is
no
going
back

One of the Innocents

The end
of
the world
again
and
those
children
at the wee
picnic
table
don't
even
know.

Then
all
their
heads
turn
at once
and look
at me
all
those
eyes
saying

"yes,
we do,
better
than you."

Veteran's Affairs

Fat
and
drooping
not
like
when
he was
a
fighter
a
warrior
when
he was
lean
and
ready
to
kill.

He
sits
at
the front
of
the classroom
back

against
the wall
trying
to
think
the way
all
the normal
everyday
fuckheads
do.

Precipitates

Walking home
from
the
movies
snow
just
starting
I can
taste
everything
alive
and
the songs
they
sing
dead things
too
the song
of sidewalk
the song
of awning
the lights
sweet lord
the lights
and
the dark sky
beyond.

The Lifeboat

Weary
of this
ocean
these
waves
the spray
the gulls
the sun
everywhere
the sun
is
a boot heel.

So
tired
but
worse
is
night
and
all
the things
that
bump
against
the hull
as

the moon
hides
her
head.

Keep Your Distance

Beauty
is
not
enough
if
lacking
kindness.

Cruel
beauty
has
its
place
its
place is
over there
well
the fuck
away
from me
but
still
where I
can
see
it.

Best of the Rest

Sparrows
on
a wire
like
dancers
in
the wings
like
cities
across
the ocean
like
hands
sorting
pictures
in
a
room
with
one
bed.

Day by Day

The crane
at
the side
of
the road
is
the tallest
thing
around
for
miles
and
miles.

Men
and
women
in
hard
hats
lean
against
it
like
they
own

it. They
don't
own it
they
barely
own
their
own
bodies,
but
for
a
few
minutes
they
sip
coffee
in
the morning
sun
and
don't
even
look
up.

New Blood

Keep
the
fire
going
please
Uncle
Fred
his
little
head
knew how
important
his little
hand
the thing
she used
to
drag
him
away.
She never
forgave
my
love
and
the fruit

it
would
never
bear
as though
I was
getting
away
with
something
the whole
of our
good
name
rested on
her
womb
like
a
garden
gnome
on
a
stump.
All
I
could
say
let
it

die
girl,
just
let it
die.
And
all
she
could
reply:
if it was
that
easy
I
wouldn't
hate
you.

Much of Life is Lived in Parking Lots

Gulls
wait
for
the bus
to stop
for
the bus
driver
to blast
the floor
clean
with
a
hose
a wave
of
crumbs
and
wrappers
out
the
back
no
dead cats
or
turnip tops

just
a feast
for
screaming
birds.

The driver
watches
the gulls
scrabble
picks
at a scab
on
his face
wonders
something
I
could
presume
to know
but
I
have
no
more
lies
I
must
get
in line

behind
the birds
and
hope
for
a
morsel.

Andre Drummond, Detroit Pistons

This gigantic
peanut-
headed
man
who
shoots
free
throws
like
a cat
trying
to
learn
to
say
"bicycle"
has
such
sadness
in his
eyes
even
a
dunk
that
shakes

the stanchion
seems
the act
of
a
disappointed
father.

James Harden, Houston Rockets

Is
it
a storm,
yet?
He
eurosteps
through
the
days
a
wannabe
screaming
thing and
never
never
shatters
into
pure
expectation.

Glass
in
the nuclei
the nuclei
in
sweat pants
more tragic

than
a rolled
eye
or thirty-five
foot heave:
some day
the beard
must
chin.

Rajon Rondo, Sacremento Kings

Here come
those
foreigners
again
to
fuck up
the elbow
jumper
as
if
they
knew
how
hard it was
to hit
an
elbow
jumper
all
those
parts
moving
together
boggles
the
mind.

Tell it to the Mountain

Time
to
die
like
a
lotus
sinking
like
a
lost
fawn
blinking
like
it
or
not
death
moves
and
removes
first
last
and
always
time
to

die
like
a
frost-bit
flower
like
Rutger
Hauer
like
Sunday
brunch
like
the
Wild
Bunch
like
a
Nazi
sneer
like
the
very
last
beer
like
Carmen's
nuclear
booty
like
smriti

and
shruti
oh shoot me
like
a
diamond
hibachi
like
a
gown
by
Versace
like
trying
not
to
slouch
like
a
fainting
couch
like
a
vodka
tonic
like
a
high
colonic
at

the
philharmonic
like
paint
flaking
off
the ceiling
like
"once
more
with
feeling"
like
contemplating
the horror
of the
body
while
sipping
Dom
Perignon
like
masturbating
because
you're
bored
with
the
body
slipping

toward
denouement
like
a
pair
of
cheap
shoes
like
yesterday's
news
like
a
roomful
of
babies
wailing
the
newborn
blues
like
the way
all
clocks
deny
what
is
true:
the
only

time
is
now
and
whoops
silly
cow
it's
already
over.

Born to It

Terror
is
but
a
click
away:

ruined
faces
shards
of bone
and metal
stained
concrete
animal
limbs
human
limbs
jumbled

only
a
click
away:
kittens.
Click.

Boobs.
Click.
Donate.
Click.
One
weird
trick.

Too Late Now

We
didn't
notice
the
rain
until
it
was
coming
up
through
the floor.

Ghost Story

A
trail
of
chocolate
fingerprints
along
the walls
of
the hallway
kid-
sized
kid-
height
but
I
have
no kids
myself
no
nieces
nephews
neighbors
with
young
ones
at least

that
speak
to
me.

I
scrub
I
sand
I
paint
over
the
fingerprints
they
keep
shining
through.

I
wonder
if
these
legs
are
my own
and
these
hands

how
they
float.

To Balance This Indispensable Abnegation

On
the
wire
an
apple
in
each hand
sky
above
earth
below
I
walk
and
sing:
no one
is not
a
baby
but only
you
are mine.

The Victimization of Knowledge

The bastard
elegant
headmaster
throttles
Plato
for
sport
from
spite
out of
habit
out of
fear
though
the
spotted
boys
know
most
everything
already
having
lived
through
the glorious
sprouting

of
the
mons
and
thought
not much
but
that
they
already
knew
better.

Luster

Quivering
wet
taut
skin
young
not yet
ready
to sip
from
a river
swollen
the river
of
joy
that
jumps
its
banks
pushes
cars
down
the main
drag
leaves
coffins
in

trees
not yet
keep
to
the shelf
of
bottled
water
for
now
lust
should
be
learned
in
the
shallows
as
one
can
never
stop
swimming
so
before
that
first
sup
oh
never mind

jump
in
just
try
not
to
drown.

Metic

hunted by god

nickle slots

engaged to Deborah
married to Maude

apple blossom surrender

nasty to grandma

right on the noodle

things she made that plaid
skirt do

fever dreams at cribside

pink cheeks after a dig

hints of nosophilia

back was never the same

one more dance before the cab arrives

whoever breathes equally foul

hunted by god

her sister wrote all those letters

say she can see
angels

fear the shark in the carpet

The Empress of Scott and Main

a trial of roses

watched her drown

hunted by god

the snide windows sneering

only wants fire ever-
lasting

fingers and toes

in form like a snow globe

hunted by god

in love with the mother of it all

half must hide

more than a monster

shock   she deserved much better

flight risk

hunted by god

fucking tomato seeds

a matter of speed
a matter of will

hunted by god

night widens, hell is all in

Always Back From War

in his arms I release

dog nose dog nose

the dead judge us
from their thrones

three broken ones
gather in the window
and sing

hunted by god

what crime, love?

when she loved me and
didn't
sigh so often

myopic

TONGUE

nothing real in this world

hunted by god

went bald, stayed bald

struck by the certainty, singular and pale

could sleep 'til the end

hunted by god

hunted by god

only in the dark
the stars

face turned to smoke

nothing real in this world

nothing real in this world

nothing real in this world

nothing real in this world

nothing real in this world

nothing real in this world

nothing real in this world

hunted by god

he arrests us

hunted by god   end of the wharf

anywhere but Doglick

hunted by god

Papa God Stink

driving just to drive

gate squeak really a dead rat

ouch

hunted by god

state of boiling, the skin

hunted by god   tiny little feet

the trail of dead imagined   hunted by god
every day

hunted by god

by god   hunted by god
        by god   hunted by god
    hunted by god
        hunted by god
       hunted
       hunted by god
   hunted by god
     hunted by god   hunted by god
      hunted by god   hunted
by god   hunted by god   by god
   haunted   hunted by god
       by god
     hunted by god
      hunted by god
   hunted by god   hunted
    haunted by god by god   hunted by god
    hunted by god
      hunted by god
   hunted
hunted by god hunted by god   hunted
  hunted   hunted by god
hunted by god   hunted by god
     hunted by god
   by god   hunted by god by god
    hunted by god   haunted by god
     hunted by god

MAY I BOTHER YOU FOR A FIG. GONE WEST FOR THE WINTER. STORE LEFT UNATTENDED.

1.

Crocodile floats the gutter, toothy lotus
in a downpour. Rivers call,
howl, chunder. Rivers like ravens
beg a roost. None here.

We have already lost.

2.

She is all cedar plank
and brass groove. Sister
kicks me under the table,
our boy has struck: home run!

But I cannot stop looking, her billow,
my corpse drained of want.

3.

My anus, serene and cockworthy.
Mini-soaps, shaped like seashells.
Lord, Texas is lonely.

4.

You foggy girl, I stink you!
Through the traffic circle,
through the red forest
of needles, I read your chart.

Sad faces in the lobby.
Grandma turtles,
remembers the opium den.

5.

Thighs with cream
drawn in the graveyard.

The letter "s" plucked
from the keyboard.

The bliss of the hive.

6.

Boring chicken boring Shakespeare
boring fat princess. The bell
unstruck, tossed
in the laundry basket.

7.

Jesus is fucking creepy,
a creeper, up in his tree house.
I can smell his old air jordans
all the way from Calvary.

But he looks like he'd be
a really good kisser.

8.

Ireland, I love you!
Wiggle my toes awake.
Through the glade to the brine
to the molten sea and beyond.

9.

That's a crap dragon, kid.

It's a donkey, for starters.
4-H glee club chimes:
"crap dragon, crap dragon,
bully me, I'm a sponge!"

Good donkey though, kid,

10.

Popped a soap bubble
with an engineering pencil
and ran it through the scantron.

Viscera all over the code.
A cake with a footprint in the middle.

11.

Think hard, and like a cur.
There is only win!
The shattered joints of the victor,
the mocking jay on the hedge.

12.

The prince's lips sneer,

slap meatily, glisten.
Ample hounds swarm.

The stars' grammar is scuttled,
unintelligible fire.
Murder and mercy
under red wax.

13.

When a doctor
meets a doctor,
a syndrome,
bird-shy.
Socratic
cloudburst,
this picnic
is fucked.
Drain one
abscess
and another
will bloom.
Cake hole
a synonym
for cake hole.
Doctors, listing,
sun-dried,
seed-blown.

14.

What's in the basket?
Drums and lysol.
We like to recycle.
We love it, really,
our eyeholes mulch it all.

15.

American unborn,
your résumé,
it lacks vim.
Committee that,
take the top off
and count the koi,
the drunk smears
within.

16.

I font you, do you font me?
Helvetica, you treacly bastard.
Who wears pajamas on a bike?
(your eyes say, "self-medicate,"
but your feet say to rhumba).

17.

Skeeball trebuchet
mass effect
spagnometer.
Now that right there
is some Julie Andrews-type shit.

18.

Troubling, her wee paisley neck beard.
Not many of the brethren
would care to roll through that.
We like our women as we like our time:
constant, always slipping away.

19.

The absurdity of the lime,
the innocence of the lime,
the truculence of the lime;
each has their summer.

20.

Friend, let's crush
the delicate ankles of sobriety
with an iron pipe.
Let's make the dashboard saints
avert their eyes.

21.

The bats sleep in the grotto.
Sahib's feet are hidden.

The cook polishes the scutcheon.
Everything is parallel
and will meet, someday.

22.

The pep rally:

a masterpiece of maybes.
New kicks and bloody stool
and revenue streams, huzzah!

Post-prep:
Someone forgot
        to lock the gymnasium doors.
Someone's hair is in the sink,
        not mine.

23.

Number theory number
theory grace. Prelates
awash in digitalia
point true north.
--except for bad attitude,
bent spine,
thirds. Trebly

24.

This kid just jumped me,
tried to give me a neck.
The wall got him.
Kinda felt bad,
like wiping lips
with dry old balm.

25.

The ball girl had a stroke
right in the middle of the court.
She left a lemon meme,
an itch in the sky,
the smell of moist wool.
Again, the prigs were satisfied.

26.

Mangled click tracks
and escalator juice.

Paternal hair-grease.
Inevitable clown shoes.

After dinner, wombish,
mangled click tracks on "repeat."

27.

Length. Boys lie.
Only napalm tells it straight.

28.

I am a dove, part of the frieze.
I thought the door.
One day, someone shall breathe me.
Then I will know
what doves in the sky know.

29.

He enjoyed everyone:
hipcools, danks, strummergirls,
the lazed, stink eyes,
whits. Fed coffee cake
to the vultures.
There was none better.

Too bad he is still here.

30.

They broke the cradle up
for firewood.

31.

It is a cat,
or a parody of a cat,
alone in a dream of god.

32.

Shotgun! On a night not fit
for worm or master
or snatch of song,
a fourth for bridge,
the slaughter of the innocents,
angels. No one, in wet socks.

33.

Premature in spirit,
unable to learn from
molecular shifts, fortran,
climbing the rust garden.
Hence the modern nation state,

and all ye heartless devils.

34.

Skim work off the top of golf

and boil it down til reduced by half.

The monkeys want to scratch us.

The monkeys will be ashtrays.

35.

Merit is for sheep,
merit is a laxative for sheep.
Remember, when you are prized:
mutton, sweaters,
the chef's mustache.

36.

Nice lisp.
Like to get my tongue around that.
A bag full of flies.
Buñuel's razored eye.

My sibilant hero,
how rough your hands must be!

37.

It's gonna take an ocean
of manufactured serotonin
to fill the weeping crater
and euthanize the haters.

38.

My acronym is bold,
my seats are plush.

More chrome than cheese,
more skin than giggle,
but really neither:

gathered, myself to myself,
I sway, boundless.

39.

A month of butter,
a month of bones.
Our hunger has a grandfather,
a grandmother, a clerk,
a manservant. A month of lightning.
A month of flies,
a month of skin.

40.

Abeyance!
the pink sweater said.
Canned pastry
and ham steaks for the beast.

Monday morning, sir.

41.

Twenty percent of the difference
between the sun and the moon,
standard deviation.
The crack in the plaster,
the stain on the ceiling.

42.

The plumber makes a proposal:
I will make you pavlovas
and two quarts of fresh whipped cream.

My counter-proposal:
we will spend two weeks together
in Chauvet cave.

We shook on it,
his wrist clean as milk.

43.

This word is three meters long
and five meters high.
It squats on the highway,
laughing at crows.

44.

"Skunk Bitch vs.
Turdslinger Joe."
Rabbit ears crackling,
waiting for the flag
and the snow.

45.

Salt. An aphorism.
Saltwater,
evaporation, crust, clown color spray
over green rock. A series,
tweet that sonuvabitch
right out your pepper hole.

46.

I am deeply troubled
by the absence in my life
of difficult moral decisions.
I do enjoy a popsicle
on a hot summer day.

47.

Christ, she's a boor.
Who let her pay attention to us?
I'd rather suck my own empty eyehole

than listen to her head another minute.

48.

Tenessee Ernie Ford
smiles from the wall of my basement
and it rains whiskey

and the matador dances,
his maraschino ass twitching
until sardines gather at the pier,
mouths coding binaries.

49.

Brine shrimp wearing bellhop hats.
I should get out of bed.
Nothing for the spectacular.
That toe seems broken, that one too.

50.

Quetzal, quetzal,
whet my cock,
put it on the chopping block.

Spaetzle, spaetzle,
hoof and horn,
wishing I had stayed unborn.

51.

The clock radio klaxon
is what roses smell while they sleep
and dream that upon
the legs of a millipede

they run across the sky.

52.

God the purple-faced paperweight has failed.
Papers everywhere, fat flat snowbirds.
Glad
I left the window open.

53.

So many slogans flashing so fast I
flutter of moth wings
I am the light.

54.

Muscles glisten like a sack of oily tumors,

The bed is too soft.
The bed is too hard.

The dog that never barks is howling at the wall.

55.

Terror
my tongue
a category
still warm
Unranked, yet
full of stars.

56.

I believe you. The carnival adheres to one.
To the endless things, I, too, cleave.

No right of refusal,
we must, anyway,
though the roof caves.

Save me.

THE SOUND OF ROCK SCRAPING ROCK MAY BE THE DOOR OPENING TO RELEASE US OR IT COULD BE POOR OLD EARTH CASTING OFF HER MANTLE

57.

Poetry

like trying to drive a baseball
through the window of a moving train
with a Louisville Slugger

from the outside.

58.

Sneak in naked
and pretend to look for thieves,

crenellations, dot dot dot

59.

Elegy:
Quit whilst ahead
(won a prize).

60.

Do the monkey,

do the monkey,
do the monkey,
do the monkey,
do the monkey
with me.

61.

Consumed with bitterness,
hence the hairstyle.

62.

Crowds are a tyranny.

Never mind.

63.

When my headstone goes wonky
and lists southward:

come to me, my dove.

64.

I
told lies
to everyone
and

look, that cloud
is ready.

65.

Warm sangria
a rainy day

the dogs on the porch
puzzled by a moth.

66.

Those squirrels fight all day, up the tree,
down the tree. I heard snow falling
in my half-dream.

67.

His chest like greasy old moccasins.

68.

The only thing
is being poor.

69.

In creaky chair, the spider,
a kind of throttle.

70.

He hunts who? Well, let him go.
So dreary when no one follows.

71.

Stumped! And a child,
the sea
is

72.

So many people.
So many, we are a bird, are a branch.

73.

Small town fraud,
toadstools on a log,
polly-wolly doodle all the day.

74.

Every crack, every step:
Hades averted,
balloons in the blue blue sky.

75.

Her ruined fingers cradle the can of beer.

76.

Old strawberries and new peaches
fleur-de-lys wallpaper
the snoring maid.

77.

Trilobytic chaff
in the the toes of a stone faun.

78.

Lavender and melon, baptism in the rinse sink.

79.

Immediate access: you whore.

80.

Fatigue
the blazing
nasturtiums.

81.

His face a tattered flag, the 8 ball drops.

82.

The war is over, and on a Friday!

83.

Kind of a dick
powerpoint
free coffee.

84.

Trying to wean myself off white people.

85.

I think it was a squirrel.

86.

Filthy trucker hat
chorus of fireflies.

87.

No money, no TV.

88.

No one understands how condescending they are.

89.

A little bit of fat, little bit of smoke: underwriting.

90.

L'Internationale (virtual)

the hammer (virtual)
the feeding tube.

91.

I will never go to Tonga.
She will never go to Tonga.
No one in this room.

92.

Odd numbers are preferable. Birds, shelving, whatever.

IMMEDIATELY FOLLOWING A CASCADE, STACK,
OVERFLOW, GUSH AND PREEN LIKE A GIANT BABY
BORN INTO PRIVILEGE (OR SO I IMAGINE), OF A
CHURCH SOCIAL THAT WAS NEITHER

93.

At the coronation
I fell
upon myself

a drone
spilling
carnage
remote controlled
still somehow
fungal

the cake
shuddered
sweating
summer
no baby cakes
sprouted

it was a terror
averted

all those

days we
dully
stare
at
the unexploded
world.

Tables bedecked with the frosted and the sauced moored
beneath every available tree, sparkling between them
the rocket trails of children, sticky hands on wobbly
necks and knees, they'd all seemed so breakable, as
though you could squeeze a little head between your
palms until it burst and the sugar flecked notes of a song
they'd never heard gushed forth, "Oh Lady Be Good,"
soaking your shirt. Little shoes, little dresses, little short
pants, in the big oak sheltering the cupcakes I see Ella
Fitzgerald reach down and coax a babe into her hand,
bite into his skull like a sugar cookie.

The Deacon's
brother's
wife's
hair
I did that.

Thunder!

To cars

or the chapel.
Hands
and neck
smell
of the smokehouse.

I could
nest here
forever

but doves
will not
leave us
be.

94.

Terror and tasty
flood of nerve

enough adrenalin
to hoist her
over the parapet.

95.

I play chin music
and not baseball.

96.

The prince is a worm,
everyone, the whispering earth.

97.

That not all humanity
likes ice cream?
World out of balance
I scream
"We All!"

98.

Her legs gone.
Who was driving.
Sandwiches, shoe in the road.

99.

Rebar, crumbs of concrete,
lineage—now come here
and sit on my lap,
murderess.

100.

Invite
me

home
I
am incapable.

101.

Automata, this world and the next and the next and the
next.

102.

Scrub and rinse,
apple, lavender, in the mirror,
lips:
pedicabo ego vos et irrumabo.

103.

Do you believe in magic?
Stupid question.
They're all stupid questions.

104.

Set my eyes in the muffin tin.
Break and scatter my bones,
all across the linoleum.
Like Grandma would say,
"A good day."

105.

Run away!
The zoo is on the outside,
the cage surrounds me.
But the soft music.

106.

How close, Magic Kingdom.
How magical
through the telescope.

107.

The cop is on the porch
looking at photos of a cat.

BLISS

108.

Tough stuff to get
        a terrified town
                thin sun and power lines
        one bar, one diner
blue and bitter and
        gets you so gone
                gathers like a cold wind
        bits of prairie self
in snarls enfolding
        bitter at soul's mouth
                the medicine
        the medicine sellers
just trying to get by
        that old saw
                the wind sits judgment
        the wind's throne.
Friends and friends of friends
        late cloud folding into light
                howling mouths of bottles
        surrounded by the border
we ride
        we sound out words with our mouths
                we ride
        clouds folding to the east

we follow the tail lights
       friends of friends holding tight
to the medicine.
       The moon melts away
              stumbles off the shoulder
creeps through the corn.

Billy's father's barn
       bats sputter in the yellow light
              grain alcohol grape kool aid
       carry on my wayward son shit
always the same songs
       same sad jokes sad
              someone gets a headful of lightning
       someone else sleeps in the hayloft
all night all night
       noses weep fire
              eyes itch in morning light
more time always more time.

Twenty years tore the fence down
       found Billy's secret spot
              stuck a finger in it
       didn't make it twenty years
nor Bella not Zeke nor Big Tom
       twenty years for the rest of us
              remade cell by cell
       cell learning from cell
all the same secrets
       the formula for failure

for an ass-scrubbed diner seat
for crass nativities nodding homeward
the christmas drunk
for myself no secret
and no sympathy
and certainly no ardor
motel fumble moan
and his wife at home.

Billy bought the right ticket
I can't never could ride
I lie Billy knew nothing
Billy made a sad joke sad.
Said the only song of love
anyone ever
and that was enough.

NEVER BUY PANTS ON THE INTERNET AS THOUGH ANYONE YOU WOULD CARE TO HAVE THAT TYPE OF THING CLOSE TO YOUR PARTS

109.

Heaven   whiskey   hole
begin
        a draft   over my grave
another glass a lens peer through to
floor
        night.

110.

The breadth of the coma
once the coma is over.

111.

A sack of baubles   for me sweetie.
Baubles for everyone.
        Mountains of baubles.   Avalanches   for me
sweetie.

112.

Clowntime for cops.

Dancing in their underwear,
the sign says:

It's all in the wrist.

113.

Dead lords
        lain end to end
                from here to Gehenna.

114.

Mr. Frank took the cover off the pool
and all the roses turned an ashy gray.
He also owns a motorboat.

115.

His face froze
            atop Mount Great Shit
                    eyes burnt open
                    one vision
        callous
singular.   And the birds muttered
into their breasts.

116.

I'll be here 'til the bulldozers leave.

Until they arrive, maybe.

117.

Oh, a bucket full of beetles, tipping,

spilling forth like a river of hair.

27 days since our last accident.

118.

Mother indulged me,

mother died,

my shampoo smells the same,

I have stories.

119.

Too serious, in the mirror,
too grave, not a pun.　　　　What the dead want
　　　　　　　　　　　is to not be dead.
　　　　　　　　　　　　　　　　Clean,
nothing cleaner.
　　　　　　　　　　Tears carry filth.
Tears are sewer runoff.

120.

Coffins look so uncomfortable
so inelegant.

And everyone will say
"what a nice service."

Pski's Porch Publishing was formed July 2012, to make books for people who like people who like books. We hope we have some small successes.
www.pskisporch.com.

Pski's Porch
323 East Avenue
Lockport, NY 14094
www.pskisporch.com

www.ingramcontent.com/pod-product-compliance
Lightning Source LLC
Chambersburg PA
CBHW060335050426
42449CB00011B/2762